Scales

by Jennifer Boothroyd

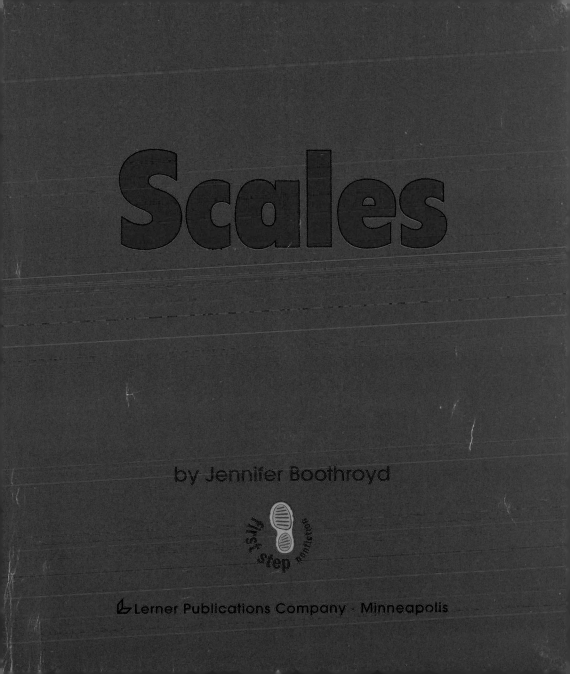

first step nonfiction

Lerner Publications Company · Minneapolis

Scales are pieces of hard
skin on the outside of an
animal's body.

2

Many animals have scales.

Fish have scales.

Reptiles have scales.

Snakes are reptiles.

Lizards are reptiles.

Many reptiles live in hot places.

Their scales keep them from drying out.

Snakes **shed** their old skin
and scales.

Some scales are thick and
rough.

Others are shiny and soft.

Many scales are flat and smooth.

13

Scales **protect** animals.

Spiky scales keep away
hunting animals.

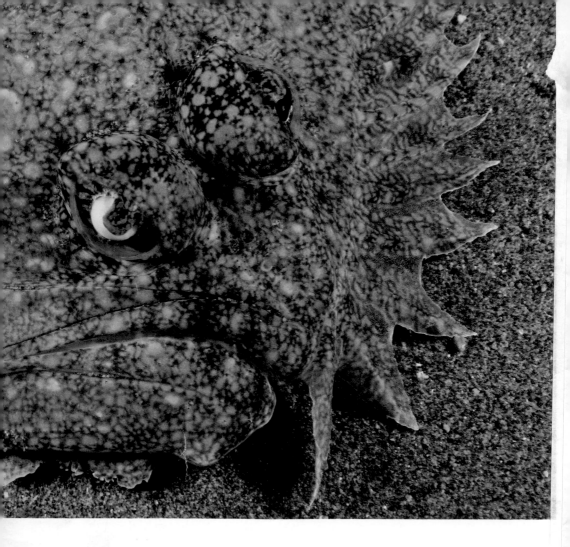

Scales help animals hide.

Scales help animals **survive**
in their surroundings.

17

Inside Out

Snakes need to shed their old scales and skin. A snake will scratch its head on something hard. The old skin peels back over its head. The snake scrapes and slithers until all the old skin comes off. It takes about two weeks for a snake to shed its skin.

Old skin peels back

Snake slithers out of skin

Skin peels off for two weeks

Facts about Scales

 People can tell the age of some fish by looking at their scales.

 Scales are made of keratin. Human fingernails are made of the same material.

 Snakes do not have eyelids. Clear scales cover their eyes.

 Sharks have very tightly connected scales. Shark skin looks smooth. It feels rough like sandpaper.

 Crocodiles have thick, hard scales called scutes.

 Dry, thick scales are at the end of a rattlesnake's tail. They make a rattling sound.

 A pangolin is an unusual mammal. (A mammal has hair and drinks its mother's milk.) A pangolin's body is covered with thin keratin scales. It is the only mammal with these scales.

Glossary

 protect – to keep safe

 reptiles – cold-blooded animals that crawl or slither

 scales – hard skin on an animal's body

 shed – to lose or fall off

 survive – to keep living

Index

The images in this book are used with the permission of: © Patricio Robles Gil/Minden Pictures, p. 2; © Jeff Hunter/Photographer's Choice/Getty Images, p. 3; © Michael Gray/Dreamstime.com, p. 4; © Tier Und Naturfotografie J & C Sohns/Workbook Stock/Getty Images, pp. 5, 22 (second from top); © Pete Oxford/Minden Pictures, pp. 6, 22 (third from top); © Alexander Safonov/ Flickr/Getty Images, p. 7; © Poco_bw/Dreamstime.com, p. 8; © Uryandrikov Sergey/Shutterstock Images, p. 9; © Michael & Patricia Fogden/Minden Pictures, pp. 10, 22 (fourth from top); © Heidi & Hans-Juergen Koch/Minden Pictures, p. 11; © Freedomman/Dreamstime.com, p. 12; © Norman Price/Alamy, p. 13; © imagebroker.net/SuperStock, pp. 14, 22 (top); © Joe McDonald/Visuals Unlimited, Inc., p. 15; © Brandon Cole, p. 16; © David Fleetham/Visuals Unlimited, Inc., pp. 17, 22 (bottom); © John Cancalosi/Alamy, p. 19 (top); © age fotostock/ SuperStock, p. 19 (middle); © Animals Animals/SuperStock, p. 19 (bottom).
Front Cover: © Nata-Lia/Shutterstock Images (background); © Tischenko Irina/Shutterstock Images (goldfish).

Main body text set in ITC Avant Garde Gothic 21/25. Typeface provided by Adobe Systems.

Lerner Publications Company
A division of Lerner Publishing Group, Inc.
241 First Avenue North
Minneapolis, MN 55401 U.S.A.

Website address: www.lernerbooks.com

Library of Congress Cataloging-in-Publication Data

Boothroyd, Jennifer, 1972–
    Scales / by Jennifer Boothroyd.
        p.   cm. — (First step nonfiction — Body coverings)
    Includes index.
    ISBN 978–0–7613–5787–2 (lib. bdg. : alk. paper)
    1. Scales (Fishes)—Juvenile literature. 2. Scales (Reptiles)—Juvenile literature. I. Title.
QL942.B664 2012
591.47'7—dc22   2010050650

Manufactured in the United States of America
1 – PC – 7/15/11